CONTENTS

What's the problem?	4
WWF then and now	6
How does WWF help?	8
Meet Nazir Foead – project worker	10
Meet Jenny Waldron – WWF volunteer	12
Meet Jim Kitchen – regional organizer	14
Meet Elizabeth Davis – supporter care worker	16
Working on projects	18
Work in education	20
Work in campaigning	22
Work in fund-raising	24
New discoveries	26
Vision for the future	28
What you can do	30
Glossary	31
Index	32

WHAT'S THE PROBLEM?

We live in a world of deep oceans, breathtaking mountain peaks, vast deserts and glorious rainforests. These stunning landscapes are home to proud animals, soaring birds, strange sea creatures and much, much more. Yet all around the world, plants, animals and the natural **environment** in which they and we live are under threat.

▼ **At the beginning of the 20th century there were 100,000 tigers – now there are only about 5000 left worldwide.**

UNDER ATTACK

The wildlife in the world's rivers, lakes and seas is being poisoned by **pollution**, chemicals and waste poured from factories and farms on land, and ships and oil rigs at sea. Forest creatures find themselves homeless when trees are chopped down to clear land for farms or houses. Natural **habitats** such as woodlands, marshes and **coral reefs** are being destroyed by human activity.

Many of the animals, plants and natural environments which are being ravaged are unique. If rare creatures like the tiger are allowed to become **extinct**, or precious habitats like the tropical forests are destroyed, they can never be replaced or recreated.

▶ **Magical underwater creatures like this jewel anemone are under threat from pollution.**

Humans have destroyed more than 30% of the natural world since 1970.

WWF

LOUISE SPILSBURY

Heinemann
LIBRARY

H **www.heinemann.co.uk**
Visit our website to find out more information about **Heinemann Library** books.

To order:
☎ Phone 44 (0) 1865 888066
📄 Send a fax to 44 (0) 1865 314091
💻 Visit the Heinemann Bookshop at www.heinemann.co.uk to browse our catalogue and order online.

First published in Great Britain by Heinemann Library, Halley Court, Jordan Hill, Oxford OX2 8EJ, a division of Reed Educational and Professional Publishing Ltd.
Heinemann is a registered trademark of Reed Educational & Professional Publishing Ltd.

OXFORD MELBOURNE AUCKLAND JOHANNESBURG BLANTYRE
GABORONE IBADAN PORTSMOUTH NH (USA) CHICAGO

© Reed Educational and Professional Publishing Ltd 2001.
Published in association with WWF–UK. The moral right of the proprietor has been asserted.

Designed by Ken Vail Graphic Design, Cambridge
Originated by Universal Colour Scanning
Printed by Wing King Tong in Hong Kong

Heinemann Library paid a contribution to WWF for their help in the creation of this book.

ISBN 0 431 0 2735 8 (hardback)   ISBN 0 431 02741 2 (paperback)
05 04 03 02 01   05 04 03 02 01
10 9 8 7 6 5 4 3 2 1   10 9 8 7 6 5 4 3 2 1

British Library Cataloguing in Publication Data
Spilsbury, Louise
WWF. – (Taking Action!)
1.World Wide Fund for Nature – Juvenile literature
I.Title
361.7'63'0941

Acknowledgements
The Publishers would like to thank WWF–UK and WWF International for supplying all the photographs used in this book.

Cover illustration by Scott Rhodes.

Every effort has been made to contact copyright holders of any material reproduced in this book. Any omissions will be rectified in subsequent printings if notice is given to the Publisher.

Words appearing in the text in bold, **like this**, are explained in the Glossary.

If we want to enjoy views like this one of a waterfall in Scotland, we need to take action to protect the world's wild places and wildlife.

Cities cover only 2% of the world's land surface but use 75% of its *natural resources.*

WWF THEN AND NOW

The World Wide Fund For Nature (WWF) was set up in 1961 by a small group of wildlife enthusiasts. They included Sir Julian Huxley, a famous British **biologist**, Peter Scott, the **naturalist** and painter, and Max Nicholson, also a naturalist. They had been appalled by the destruction of **habitats** and wildlife in Africa. They feared that much of the region's wildlife was in danger of being wiped out – and that similar dangers faced the rest of the world.

The **charity's** first members were scientists and people who knew how to get information about WWF into the **media**. The charity's aim was to find out where the problems were and to let people around the world know what those problems were.

▼ **The WWF panda logo was designed by Sir Peter Scott, who was one of the founding members of the charity in 1961. The big, furry animal with its appealing, black-patched eyes is instantly recognizable all over the world.**

◄ **WWF founders Sir Julian Huxley (left) and Max Nicholson (right) in Coto Doñana, Spain, an important wildlife *reserve*, in 1970.**

WWF has national organizations in 27 countries across the world.

WWF TODAY

Since then, WWF has grown to become the largest **conservation** and environmental organization in the world. Today it is a network of national organizations with representatives in more than 50 countries across the world. WWF International is based in Switzerland. This head office co-ordinates the other WWF organizations and offices around the world. The national organizations carry out conservation work in their own countries and many also operate all over the world. They all provide funds for WWF International and help with WWF's international **campaigns**. They also advise local, national and international organizations on how to deal with environmental problems. In countries where there is no national organization, WWF links up with independent local organizations so it can continue its work.

The WWF Programme Office in Indonesia became the 27th National Organization in June 1998.

7

WWF has around 5 million supporters across the world.

HOW DOES WWF HELP?

Whatever the time of day, whatever the season, somewhere in the world WWF is working to protect the natural world and the people who live in it. In countries all over the world, WWF scientists and researchers are working to find out which **habitats** or living things are most in need of help. Then WWF experts work with local people and organizations to come up with realistic, cost-effective, long-term solutions to those problems.

ACROSS THE WORLD

Overseas, WWF helps to protect many **endangered species**, including the tiger, rhino, turtle and whale. WWF also works to save precious habitats including mountains, **coral reefs**, **wetlands**, forests and coasts. Much of the **charity's** work is about finding ways to protect the **environment** while caring for the needs of the people who live in it. WWF helps people find ways of living and supporting themselves which do not threaten wildlife or wild places. It also shows them ways in which they can actually benefit by working on **conservation**.

Across the world WWF works with people to help them improve their lives while protecting their environment at the same time.

Since 1961 WWF has funded almost 3000 conservation projects in the UK.

WWF-UK

WWF works throughout the UK on land, freshwater and sea issues. WWF-UK also works closely with WWF offices in Europe.

WWF-UK plays an important role in influencing government decisions that affect our natural environment. One way in which WWF-UK achieves this is by using scientific research to persuade the government to change laws that allow damage to be done to the environment.

WWF-UK also works to save endangered species, restore damaged wildlife habitats and protect areas of natural beauty all over the country.

 WWF-UK pays for projects to restore and protect Britain's wild places.

WWF Scotland is a leading force in WWF's International Arctic Programme, working with eight countries to protect the fragile environment in which animals like this polar bear live.

WWF has set up 12,600 conservation projects in 154 countries.

MEET NAZIR FOEAD
PROJECT WORKER

In the last three years, I have been working to protect Javan rhinos living in the Ujung Kulon **National Park**, Indonesia. My team and I study the animals and work on other rhino **conservation** activities with local people who live around the Park.

The forest is very thick and the rhinos are hard to spot. We keep a check on rhino numbers and identify individuals using photos taken by special cameras. We also check on the rhino population by collecting rhino droppings. By studying the **genetic analysis** of the droppings we can tell lots of important things about the rhinos, such as which ones are from the same family. Our plan is to increase the number of Javan rhinos in the Park.

▲ **The Javan rhino is a huge, lovely animal. A few Javan rhinos are found in Vietnam, but most of them live in Ujung Kulon National Park.**

6am Our first job is to prepare our food for the whole day and sort out the gear we need for a day collecting rhino droppings.

8.50am After two hours walking in the forest, we find a place where rhinos like to wallow. We find a few footprints, but no droppings. Judging from the week-old tracks, two different rhinos wallow here. We follow the footprints for an hour but the tracks disappear. We try looking further north-east.

WWF operates 30 rhino conservation programmes in Africa and Asia.

12noon A friend at the front of the group suddenly calls out — he's found a rhino dropping. It's huge, almost 60 cm wide. We make notes about our position, the time and the kind of plants in the area. We also take a picture, and slice off a small piece of the dropping to study later.

1pm After lunch, I leave the team and head west, for an important meeting in one of the villages near the Park. This involves a long walk through a forest full of biting mosquitoes and a muddy motorbike-taxi ride.

5.30pm At the village two other WWF workers fill me in on the plans for the meeting.

7.30pm At the meeting we talk to the villagers about how they can help with rhino conservation. We agree that they need help to earn enough money so that they do not need to take **natural resources**, such as wood, from the Park. We plan more meetings to sort out what help the villagers need, who will provide that help, and what the villagers will do to protect the Park.

▲ **The collection team scoop up a sample of the rhino dropping.**

▼ **These women from the village are using ginger to make a special drink which they can sell to support themselves.**

11

There are only 65 Javan rhinos left in the world.

MEET JENNY WALDRON
WWF VOLUNTEER

I've been interested in wildlife since I was seven years old. Now I'm a **volunteer** with the local Poole and Dorset WWF group. One of the things I do is to help WWF raise money to protect **endangered species** and their **habitats** in the UK and across the world. I also visit schools and other organizations to talk about the importance of **conservation** and to encourage people to take action themselves to improve our **environment**. I'm even involved in research and get the chance to study local sea life, particularly dolphins and seals.

10am I head for the cliffs at Swanage, where I'm doing two hours' 'dolphin watch'. This is part of a WWF project to keep an eye on the number and health of the dolphins in our area.

11.30am I spot a dolphin. I contact the Marine Project Officer by radio from the cliffs. She heads off in her boat to photograph the dolphin and make notes about it. She writes down where the dolphin was seen, what other wildlife is in the area, and what boat traffic is about.

12 noon Just before I leave, a group of schoolchildren on a nature walk stop to ask me about the wildlife in the area and what WWF is doing to protect it.

▼ **Dolphins are one of my favourite animals. It's a real pleasure to be involved in protecting these wonderful creatures.**

Thousands of dolphins die every year when they are caught up in long fishing nets.

12.30pm Today another volunteer, Cathryn, and I are planning a 'birthday party' for Lumpy, one of the dolphins regularly seen off our coast. We've invited some local schoolchildren. As well as having fun, they'll learn a lot about sea life at the party.

2pm I visit a school in Poole to give a talk on wildlife and what WWF does. I also talk about the environment and why we need to look after it. I show some pictures and slides to explain to the children what I mean.

6pm We have a local group meeting to discuss fund-raising events. We're planning a fashion show (with second-hand clothes), a **sponsored** walk, a jumble sale and a fête in the coming months! We're also working on some educational events with local companies and the council to advise them on things that they can do to protect and improve the environment. It's been a busy but really satisfying day.

At the birthday party for Lumpy the dolphin I wore my special suit made out of waste material. I reminded the children that when they're on a picnic they should never give food to any animals and that they must always take their rubbish home or put it in a dustbin.

The rarest marine mammal in the world is the Yangtze River dolphin – there are only 150 left.

MEET JIM KITCHEN
REGIONAL ORGANIZER

Every year thousands of children like you take part in WWF's 'Walk for Wildlife'. These walks raise a lot of money to help WWF protect the world's wild places and the wonderful creatures that live in them. As regional organizer in Belfast it's my job to help arrange and support events like these in Northern Ireland.

Earlier this year I visited Africa to find out how WWF spends the money that I help to raise. In Tanzania, WWF helps communities to look after the tropical forests. The **charity** also helps and encourages people there to protect **endangered species**, such as the beautiful black rhino.

7am Today is the annual 'Walk for Wildlife' day. I'm making an early start because I want to visit as many of the 16 walks going on in Northern Ireland as possible. All of the walks are organized by WWF **volunteers**, and as well as meeting the walkers I want to thank the organizers for all their hard work.

9am I arrive at Portrush on the north coast, where over 120 children from local schools are walking along 8 km of sandy beach. They are all walking well and I thank them for their support.

Here I am with a women's group in Tanzania. I had a chance to talk to them about how they look after the trees in their local forest.

14

In the UK about 15,000 people take part in WWF's 'Walk for Wildlife' events.

At Belfast Zoo i spend some time answering children's questions about the animals there.

11.30am It's much calmer inland at Randalstown Forest, where red squirrels and fallow deer are watching the walkers from the woodland. I join a group on the shore of Lough Neagh, the UK's largest freshwater lake, to watch the ducks swimming in the bay.

1.30pm The animals are more exotic at the next stop — Belfast Zoo. Here WWF funds a breeding programme to return golden lion tamarins, which are delightful little monkeys, to their native forest in Brazil.

4pm Last stop is Crawfordsburn, where WWF volunteers are greeting the last few walkers arriving at the finish line. I talk to a journalist from BBC Radio Ulster, who wants to know about how the walks are helping WWF's overseas projects.

6pm The results are coming in from all of the events. Over 700 people have been out walking for wildlife in Northern Ireland today. I'm really pleased and I make lots of telephone calls to thank the organizers for all their help.

These schoolchildren walked 6 km for WWF. They had a great day out and raised money to help the world's wildlife too!

In the 20th century 134 *species* of plants and animals became *extinct* in the UK.

MEET ELIZABETH DAVIS
SUPPORTER CARE WORKER

9am WWF has just launched a story about the Iberian lynx, the world's most endangered cat, which has fallen in number by half in the last ten years. The story has appeared in some newspapers so I'll be answering lots of calls about this during the day.

10.30am A supporter telephones because he is going on holiday and wants some advice about holiday souvenirs. I tell him that illegal wildlife souvenirs include any alligator or crocodile items, elephant ivory, coral, live plants, live parrots, queen conch shells and live reptiles. I send him a WWF leaflet so he knows which products to avoid.

Hello, my name is Elizabeth and I work in the head office of WWF-UK. I really like my job because I always wanted to work for WWF. I like the idea of working for a **charity** that strives to protect the **environment**, **endangered species** and their **habitats**.

My job involves working with the fund-raising department. I answer questions, and occasionally deal with complaints, from WWF supporters. It's important to keep our supporters happy so that they go on helping WWF, and to keep up our reputation as a charity that really cares.

> **Leaflets like this tell tourists which products to avoid when buying holiday souvenirs.**

Wherever you travel spare a thought for the local wildlife

Think twice before you buy souvenirs

Souvenirs made from animal skins, tortoiseshell, ivory or coral are illegal – and kill animals.

11.45am A supporter calls to adopt an animal for a friend's birthday present. She chooses to adopt Kinyanjui, a black rhino. By paying a small amount each month she'll be helping to protect Kinyanjui and other rhinos from being killed by hunters who sell their horns. Her friend will receive a certificate saying she has adopted him, a photograph and newsletters about his progress throughout the year.

3pm I go to a special meeting with the rest of the supporter care team. A project worker from WWF-Malaysia has come to tell us about its work to protect orang-utans there. This is really interesting and it's important for me to know all about WWF projects when supporters call in for information.

4.30pm A supporter calls because she's worried about a shawl she's seen for sale. She has heard that up to five Tibetan antelope are killed just to make one Shahtoosh shawl. The demand for these shawls is increasing, and the antelopes are an endangered species. I tell her WWF is doing all we can to protect these creatures.

5.15pm Before I go home I clear my desk and sort out all my waste into the recycling bins. If you care about the environment recycling is vital!

> **I use my computer a lot. It's a quick and easy way of finding up-to-date information.**

> **I'm very interested in the talk about orang-utans because the orang-utan is one of my favourite animals.**

There are only 30,000 orang-utans left in the wild.

WORKING ON PROJECTS

We all rely on the natural world for life – for the air we breathe, the food we eat, the medicines that make us better, and many of the fuels we use for heating, cooking and lighting. It is vitally important that whenever any of us, anywhere in the world, uses the Earth's **natural resources**, we use them in a way which is **sustainable**. This means in ways which do not use them up to the point where there is not enough to go round, or to the point where they run out altogether. This is why, when WWF works on projects to protect the natural world, one of its first considerations is the people who share that **environment**.

WWF projects work with individuals, local communities, governments, and other **conservation** groups to find ways of taking action to protect and improve the environment together.

Across the world WWF works with local people to find long-term, practical solutions to problems. In Cameroon, children are planting new trees, to keep forests alive.

These schoolchildren are at a conservation centre in Wales helping WWF monitor bird boxes. They are counting the number of birds that use the boxes to find out how many birds are living there.

In the 20th century half of the world's tropical forests were destroyed.

In the Solomon Islands in the South Pacific, people rely on fishing to earn a living. WWF is working with community groups to find ways of preventing overfishing (when fish stocks run out).

In Brazil's Atlantic Forest WWF is working with local people to find ways of protecting their environment and studying the plants and wildlife there.

There are 8 million *species* of animals and plants in the world.

WORK IN EDUCATION

Almost every decision we make and every action we take – at home, school, work, or on holiday – has an effect on the natural world. WWF's work in education helps people understand and care about the way they and others in their communities treat their **environment**. It also encourages people to think about how the things they do affect other people, locally and across the world.

IN SCHOOLS

WWF produces all sorts of books, posters and teachers' packs to bring environmental issues into the classroom. It is important that environmental issues are not just discussed in science lessons, because the environment is a part of all aspects of our lives. So WWF makes materials for all ages and for every subject in the school curriculum – from history to home economics. It also runs a website that has up-to-date information on all the latest environmental issues (www.wwf-uk.org).

WWF used its links with Nigeria to produce a series of history books about Benin, an ancient African kingdom. As well as describing the region's history, WWF was able to examine how people in the past lived without damaging their environment.

WWF is one of the biggest producers of environmental education resources in the UK.

IN THE COMMUNITY

WWF works with local community groups and organizations to organize projects together. For example, **recycling** schemes help keep pavements clean, and by reducing waste they help to stop the depletion of the world's **natural resources**. By creating new gardens, communities not only encourage butterflies and other wildlife, they also improve the look and feel of the environment for everyone to enjoy.

ACROSS THE WORLD

As well as sharing its ideas and experience with schools and communities in other countries across the world, WWF also works with different religious groups. Nearly three-quarters of the world's people follow a religion. By helping religious teachers emphasize the environmental messages in their educational books, WWF is able to get its important message onto more streets and villages than ever before.

◀ **Learning is not just something we do in school. We go on learning all our lives. WWF works to teach people of all ages what they can do to protect the natural world.**

▶ **WWF produces lots of different kinds of education resources about the natural world, including books, tapes, stories and jigsaw puzzles.**

WWF takes action to protect the environment for people and nature.

WORK IN CAMPAIGNING

Campaigns are a way of telling people what difficulties animals and the natural world face. Campaigns explain what WWF is doing to help, and they make people aware of what they can do – either by donating money to WWF or by taking action themselves. WWF-UK concentrates on two main campaigns a year. For example, in 1999 these were the Living Countryside Campaign and the Campaign for Europe's Carnivores.

▼ **Thousands of WWF supporters joined forces to campaign outside Parliament for new countryside laws in 1999.**

LIVING COUNTRYSIDE CAMPAIGN

This campaign covers a number of different projects to protect the countryside in the UK. Its aim is to increase the number of **habitats** and threatened **species** that are protected by law. WWF then works with local authorities and governments to ensure that this protection is carried out.

One of the campaign's most important aims is to rescue damaged habitats. In Cambridgeshire, for example, WWF is working with local people to restore an area of marshland. They are trying to work out how to stop the serious loss of species which is happening there as habitats are lost when land is concreted over for buildings or taken for farmland. WWF hopes that one day there will be an even wider range of wildlife than lives there now.

The loss of forests in northern Europe is destroying bear habitats and their food supplies

CAMPAIGN FOR EUROPE'S CARNIVORES

This campaign was launched in 1999 to make people aware of **endangered species** such as wolves, bears and the Iberian lynx. These are European **carnivores** that may become **extinct** within the next 50 years.

One of the hardest parts of this campaign is persuading people in northern Europe that they can live near large carnivores such as bears and wolves. Lots of us have grown up hearing stories about big bad wolves and hungry bears and are frightened by these creatures. But the stories are often untrue.

In the Carpathian Mountains in Romania, WWF has been using leaflets, educational visits to schools, and reports in the **media** to teach people that carnivores are a natural part of their mountainous landscape and not to be feared. WWF has also developed a tourist project to encourage people to visit the area to see the wildlife in groups which take care not to disturb either the animals or the **environment**. This is benefiting the local people as the tourists bring money into the town.

To help endangered carnivores like these bear cubs WWF must understand how they survive. So they trap them and fit them with radio collars so they can monitor what they do and where they go.

Who's afraid of the big bad wolf? In North America, which has far more wolves than northern Europe, no one has been killed by a wolf for over 100 years, whereas many wolves have been killed by people. Who's really in danger here?

The Iberian lynx is the most threatened cat species in the world – now down to a mere 800.

WORK IN FUND-RAISING

One of the important things which **campaigns** do is to tell people why WWF needs their money. As a **charity** WWF relies on money donated by people like you to carry out its important work. Without it, WWF would not be able to continue to protect the natural world.

Supporters all over the UK and the rest of the world give their time and effort in all sorts of ways to raise money for WWF. Some members hold **sponsored** swims, runs, or bike rides.

Every year thousands of people all over the UK take part in WWF's 'Walk for Wildlife' and raise money for the charity. **Volunteers** also collect money in collection tins in shops, schools and in the street. Some people leave money to WWF in their wills. On New Year's Eve 1999 people lit 3000 beacons across the UK to celebrate the new millennium and to raise money for charities, including WWF.

These WWF supporters took part in 'The Great WWF Shark Swim' to raise funds in May 1999.

Humans kill an estimated 100,000,000 sharks a year, while sharks account for only 6 human deaths.

▶ **WWF produces a variety of toys, gifts and books with a wildlife theme. It sells these through a mail-order catalogue. It's a successful way of raising funds for the charity's work.**

◀ **As part of WWF's 'Adopt an animal' scheme you can help animals in danger, like these elephants. By paying a regular amount you get a photo, newsletters and a certificate of adoption. The money helps WWF to protect the animals.**

Gifts of money from individuals make up over half of WWF's yearly income.

NEW DISCOVERIES

The forests of Nha-Ke Bang in central Vietnam and Hin Namno in Laos in South-east Asia are like secret gardens. They are treasure troves of precious **endangered species** and **habitats** that have been little explored or studied. In the heart of the forest dwell the Ruc people, who live alongside the endangered tiger, leopard, black bear, and rare birds such as the great hornbill and imperial pheasant, as well as monkeys like the gibbon and langur. The forests are also home to many creatures and plants that are as yet unknown.

RARE MAMMALS

WWF is working alongside Vietnamese scientists on projects in these forests to find new **species** and to protect those that are already known about. In 1992 and 1994 WWF surveys made two very exciting discoveries. They found two new species of large **mammal** – the giant muntjac (a kind of deer) and the sao la (a kind of ox). In the 20th century fewer than ten new large mammal species were discovered worldwide, so it was even more amazing to find two species within a short time and within the same area.

The sao la (or Vu Quang ox) captured world attention when it was discovered in 1992.

WWF teams work closely with the governments of the countries in which they carry out surveys.

It seems highly likely that more new species may be found in the future. This gave WWF further proof of the need to protect and preserve the animals and their unique habitat.

RESERVES

Since these new mammals were found, the Vietnamese government has enlarged the area of land set aside for wildlife to live safely in. It has also banned the cutting down of trees that provide the habitat and food for these creatures. Hunting these animals has also been banned. A lot of people living in or near the forests relied on hunting animals like the giant muntjac for food. WWF is working with the governments in Laos and Vietnam to provide people with other sources of food and better conditions so they do not have to hunt such rare animals to live.

WWF is teaching local people about the importance of conservation and protecting the **reserve**. WWF is also helping to set up a corridor of land between the reserve in Vietnam and a similar reserve in the forests in Laos. This would mean that all the large mammals in the area could roam freely and safely between the forests.

This is Pham Mong Giao, one of the members of the team who first found skulls and other evidence of the existence of the giant muntjac.

Vietnam is home to around 275 mammal species, including tigers, elephants and rhinos.

VISION FOR THE FUTURE

WWF's vision for the future is a world in which people and nature can live together in harmony. In the future it hopes to stop, and eventually reverse the destruction which is going on today. WWF is working hard to preserve and protect the world's oceans and coasts, its many kinds of forests and freshwater **environments** and the plants and animals which live in them. These things are vital to the well-being of all life on Earth, including us.

▲ **By protecting plants and animals people will have a better chance of ensuring their own future. For example, the creation of 'no fishing' areas should stop the danger of fish we enjoy eating, like cod, becoming *extinct*.**

▼ **WWF aims to ensure that any use of *natural resources* is *sustainable*. This means that people use energy from sources like these wind turbines which do not harm the environment and which will not run out one day.**

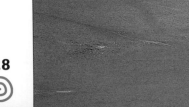

The abundance of plant and animal *species*, such as the orchid (left) and otter (below), will be protected and valued for the children of the future.

Everyone can protect our wildlife and countryside by cutting down on *pollution* and by reducing the amount of waste we all produce.

WHAT YOU CAN DO

If you care about the Earth, and the people, animals and plants that live on it, perhaps you would like to contact us and join WWF.

WWF-UK
Panda House
Weyside Park
Godalming
Surrey GU7 1XR
Tel: 01483 426444
Fax: 01483 426409
Or visit the website on:
www.wwf-uk.org

These are a few ways in which you can take action to help right now.

Encourage wildlife
by planting wild flower seeds; by putting up a bird table, bird box or even a bat box; by growing plants that attract butterflies

Help the **environment**
by never picking wild flowers, digging up dead plants or breaking tree branches; by keeping to proper tracks and paths when walking or cycling, because straying off paths disturbs wildlife and destroys plants; by respecting wildlife in ponds, pools and rock pools; by taking rubbish home

Save wildlife
by not buying souvenirs made from **endangered species** such as coral when you are on holiday; by being careful to take home hooks, lines, weights and nets if you go fishing; by never disturbing birds' nests or collecting eggs

Save fuel
by walking, cycling or using public transport when it's safe to do so; by giving friends a lift in the car if that is the only way of getting around

▼ Children at a mobile *recycling* unit in Reading – a project which WWF-UK has supported.

30

WWF has more than 255,000 members and supporters in the UK.

GLOSSARY

biologist scientist who studies living things

campaign organized activity to bring about change

carnivores animals that feed on the flesh of other animals

charity non-profit-making organization set up to help others

conservation taking action to stop rare animals and plants from dying out and to protect all other living things and the wild places in which they live

coral reefs coral is a hard substance made by living things called polyps to support and protect them. Some polyps share huge coral skeletons called reefs.

endangered species plant or animal in danger of becoming extinct

environment surroundings in which we and other living creatures live or rely upon, like seas, rivers, forests, air, or buildings

extinct plant or animal species which has died out

genetic analysis studying the genes of living things. Genes carry the information from parent to offspring in all living things that makes them the way they are.

habitats natural places where groups of plants and animals live

mammals animal group that includes humans. All mammals feed their babies on their own milk.

media newspapers, magazines, radio, television and other forms of communication

national park area of natural beauty protected by law

naturalists experts in natural history, the study of nature

natural resources materials in nature which can be used by people, such as wood, oil or coal

pollution when part of the environment is poisoned or harmed by human activity

recycling using materials or things again

reserve area of protected land where plants and animals live safely

species group of animals or plants which share the same characteristics

sponsored when people promise money for a charity for an activity such as a walk or a swim

sustainable capable of being used continuously. For example, if trees are cut down, new ones are planted so the same number is always available.

volunteers people who work without being paid

wetlands swamps and other damp areas of land

INDEX

alternative energy 28
'Adopt an animal' scheme 17, 25

bears 23, 26
birds 18, 26
butterflies 21

campaigns 7, 22, 23, 24, 31
coasts and oceans 8, 9, 28
conservation 7, 8, 10, 11, 18, 31
conservation projects 8, 9, 10, 11, 26, 27
coral reefs 4, 8

dolphins 12, 13

education 12, 13, 20, 21, 23
elephants 25, 27
endangered species 8, 9, 12, 16, 17, 23, 26, 30, 31

fishing 19, 28
forests 4, 7, 8, 18, 19, 22, 26, 27
fund-raising 12, 13, 14, 15, 24, 25

head office (Switzerland) 7
Huxley, Sir Julian 6

laws 9, 22
lynxes 16, 23

mail-order catalogue 25
marshes 4, 22
media 6, 23, 31
mountains 8

national organizations 7
natural resources 5, 11, 18, 21, 28, 31
Nicholson, Max 6

orang-utans 17
otters 29

panda logo 6
polar bears 9
pollution 4, 24, 29, 31

recycling 17, 21, 30, 31
rhinos 8, 10, 11, 14, 17, 27

scientific research 8, 9
Scott, Peter 6
seals 12
sharks 24

tigers 4, 8, 26, 27
turtles 8

volunteers 12, 13, 14, 24, 31

'Walk for Wildlife' events 14, 15, 24
wetlands 8
whales 8
wolves 23
woodlands
WWF International 7